Gibraltar

in 2 days

An easy-read travel guide to get the most from your short break

James Richardson

Published by James E Richardson (Electrical) Limited

Copyright © 2018 James Richardson

All rights reserved.

ISBN: 0-9957492-1-3
ISBN-13:   978-0-9957492-1-4

Contents

Maps

View looking south near the top cable car station

Section 1 - Introduction to Gibraltar

Gibraltar is a huge limestone rock on Spain's south coast. It is about an hour and three quarters' drive from Malaga and connected to the mainland by a low lying sandy isthmus. Morocco is only a few miles across the sea to the south. At this point the Mediterranean Sea narrows to become the Strait of Gibraltar, a narrow passage from the Mediterranean into the Atlantic Ocean.

In prehistoric times Gibraltar's extensive caves were visited by Neanderthal man. To ancient civilisations, the Strait of Gibraltar marked the end of the familiar world of the Mediterranean and a gateway to the dangers beyond. Gibraltar was known in these times as Mount Calpe. Together with the mountain Mount Abyla, across the strait in North Africa, it formed the Pillars of Hercules.

Until the eleventh century Gibraltar was mostly uninhabited. In 1068 the Islamic Moors, who held much of Spain at that time, started to fortify it against invasion by rival factions from North Africa. Centuries later, with the Moors in retreat, the Spanish reconquered southern Spain and used Gibraltar as a base to attack North Africa. Also valuable for controlling the narrow strait, Gibraltar's fortifications were gradually improved.

In 1704, during the War of the Spanish Succession, the British feared victory by the Bourbon side would lead to a Europe dominated by the French. They backed Archduke Charles, of the rival Habsburg faction, and planned to assist him by capturing Cadiz where he could make his claim to the Spanish crown. Cadiz was too heavily defended so they ended up taking Gibraltar instead.

The War of the Spanish Succession was later resolved with the Treaty of Utrecht. This recognised the Bourbon king as the ruler of Spain in return for assurances that French influence on Spain would be limited. As part of this deal the British were allowed to keep Gibraltar.

Later, the Spanish tried to reclaim the Rock, both by negotiation and military attacks. The most significant of these was the Great Siege of 1779 to 1782. During this siege, the British defenders dug an impressive tunnel system to house their cannon.

The Rock continued to remain British and developed as an important naval base. It was here that Nelson's ship, Victory, returned with his body after the battle of Trafalgar to be repaired for the journey home. During the Second World War Gibraltar's port and dockyard were critical to the war in Southern Europe and North Africa. A further 30 miles of tunnels were dug and the temporary airstrip replaced with the current runway.

After the war, Spain re-asserted its claim on Gibraltar and for many years closed the land border. Meanwhile Britain gradually introduced an element of self-determination for Gibraltar. With membership of both countries in the EU the border restrictions were relaxed.

Gibraltar is now a British Overseas Territory but its sovereignty is still disputed by Spain. Although part of the European Union, it is not part of the Customs Union. This makes it a low tax centre for online gambling and offshore banking.

For the tourist it offers a compact town with bars and restaurants, overlooked by the Rock itself which is classed as a nature reserve. As well as pleasant, but steep, walks, you can visit the tunnels, caves and various military structures. Gibraltar is also home to Europe's only wild monkeys. Superstition says that while the monkeys remain, so will the British.

How to use this book

For a short break you need to get your bearings quickly. This book will minimise wasted time when you first arrive and help you prioritise the attractions that interest you most.

Section 2 – Life in Gibraltar, describes the layout of the town. It explains currency, language, public holidays and other essentials.

Section 3 – Getting there, covers ways to reach Gibraltar. It includes an orientation map and directions to take you straight to the town centre and other attractions when you arrive.

Section 4 – Suggested itineraries, recommends the best things to do for different lengths of short break. Use these ideas as a starting point to plan your trip.

Section 5 – List of attractions, describes Gibraltar's main attractions. Use it to find locations, costs and opening hours. The photos and descriptions will help you choose which are worth your time.

Section 6 – Buses in Gibraltar, gives tips for using Gibraltar's bus service. It includes bus routes and an explanation of the ticket system.

Monkeys chilling beside St Michael's Cave

They also love vehicles

Map 1 - Overview

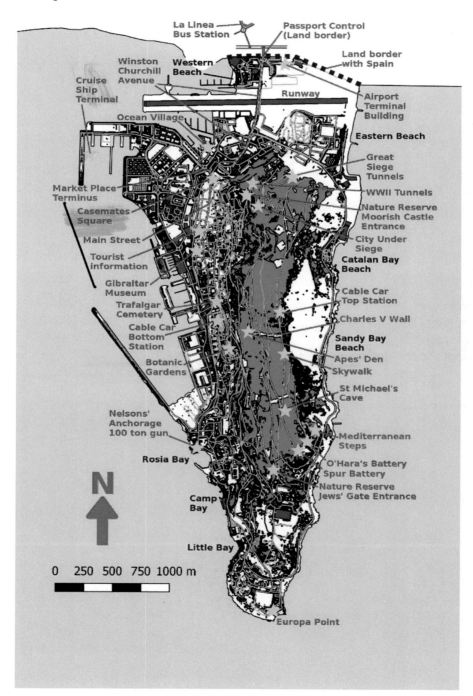

La Linea
Bus Station

Passport Control
(Land border)

Winston
Churchill
Avenue

Western
Beach

Land border
with Spain

Cruise
Ship
Terminal

Runway

Airport
Terminal
Building

Ocean Village

Eastern Beach

Great
Siege
Tunnels

Market Place
Terminus

WWII Tunnels

Casemates
Square

Nature Reserve
Moorish Castle
Entrance

Main Street

City Under
Siege

Tourist
information

Catalan Bay
Beach

Gibraltar
Museum

Cable Car
Top Station

Trafalgar
Cemetery

Charles V Wall

Cable Car
Bottom
Station

Sandy Bay
Beach

Botanic
Gardens

Apes' Den

Skywalk

St Michael's
Cave

Nelsons'
Anchorage
100 ton gun

Mediterranean
Steps

Rosia Bay

O'Hara's Battery
Spur Battery

Nature Reserve
Jews' Gate Entrance

N

Camp
Bay

Little Bay

0   250 500 750 1000 m

Europa Point

Section 2 - Life in Gibraltar

Layout

The map opposite shows the layout of Gibraltar. To the north, across the border with Spain, is the Spanish town of La Línea de la Concepción, often referred to as just La Línea. Many visitors arrive at the bus station here, two minutes' walk from the border. South of the border is Gibraltar's airport. The runway crosses the entry road and footpath. These are closed briefly when a plane takes off or lands.

From the airport and land border it is a 20 minute walk along Winston Churchill Avenue to the Market Place bus terminus. Buses and taxis are also available. The cruise ship terminal, in the north-west, is a similar distance from the Market Place terminus. Beside Market Place is Casemates Square. This open space, filled with bars and restaurants, is a major landmark when exploring the town.

From Casemates Square, Main Street runs the length of the town centre, ending at the Southport Gates. Most of the shops are aimed at tourists but you will also find the Gibraltar Museum, Tourist Information Office and Post Office. It will take at least 15 minutes to walk along Main Street, even ignoring the shops.

Continuing south through the Southport Gates at the end of Main Street, you will find the Trafalgar Cemetery, Botanic Gardens and Cable Car Bottom Station.

To the east of Main Street the town rises sharply and becomes the steep side of the Rock which leads to the Upper Rock Nature Reserve. This is the green area in the centre of the map and covers most of the high ground. Pedestrian access is at the Moorish Castle entrance, a steep climb from the northern part of Main Street or via the Jews' Gate entrance, a 30 minute uphill walk from Trafalgar Cemetery. Alternatively you could take the cable car or one of the organised taxi tours. There is also a bus to the Moorish Castle entrance.

The nature reserve is filled with attractions including caves, wartime tunnels and the only wild monkeys in Europe. Containing many hours of walks, you would struggle to see everything here in one day.

Outside of the nature reserve and town centre are a few more isolated attractions. Nelson's Anchorage displays a huge 100 ton gun, one of only two remaining of its type. Europa Point, with its lighthouse and mosque, is almost the most southerly point in Europe. Ocean Village is a trendy marina area with restaurants, bars and casinos.

Finally, if you have time to take a break from exploring, Gibraltar has a number of beaches.

Transport

There is no public transport across the frontier with Spain. You will be dropped on the Spanish side and walk through passport control on foot. Alternatively you can drive across the border in a private car.

In Gibraltar, cars drive on the right, the same as in Spain. Whether travelling on foot or by car, watch out for motorbikes which whizz round roads on both sides of the border.

Within the central area it is practical to explore on foot. To save time or travel further you can use the frequent bus service (see section 6).

There are taxi ranks outside of the airport terminal and across the road on Winston Churchill Avenue next to the border crossing. There are also ranks at Casemates Square, Trafalgar Cemetery and beside the Anglican Cathedral. You may find it hard to get a taxi as they prefer to take the more profitable Rock Tours. You could phone or email to book ahead.

Language and time

Gibraltar is in the same time zone as Spain, one hour ahead of London. English is the official language and widely understood although many people working there are Spanish.

Electricity

Mains is the same as the UK, 230 volts, 50Hz with UK style 13 amp sockets.

Telephones

The international dialling code for Gibraltar is +350. If you are coming from other parts of the European Union, any minutes and data allowance from you own country can also be used here (subject to fair use limits) and in Spain at no extra charge. You can also phone Gibraltar numbers and other EU countries using your inclusive minutes while in Gibraltar, even though calls to these countries would be charged if you were at home.

Useful Contacts:

Emergency services including police	199 or 112	EMERGENCY ONLY
Emergency (fire/ambulance only)	190	EMERGENCY ONLY

Police (non-emergency)	+350 200 72500
Fire (non-emergency)	+350 200 79507
Ambulance (non-emergency)	+350 200 77390

St Bernard's Hospital	+350 200 79700
Primary Care Centre (doctor)	+350 200 72355

Museum	+350 200 74805
Cable Car Bottom Station	+350 200 12765
Book WWII Tunnel tour	+350 200 45000 / 71643 / 71648
	email: ur&beaches@gibraltar.gov.gi

Tourist Info	+350 200 45000	information@tourism.gov.gi
Airport info desk	+350 200 12345	info@gia.gov.gi
Taxi	+350 200 70027	gibtaxiass@gibtelecom.net

Customs Restrictions and National Status

Gibraltar is a British Overseas Territory. It is not part of the EU Customs Union. For those used to crossing European borders without restriction on goods for personal use this may be a surprise. The situation at the border is like crossing into a non-EU country. There are old style duty free allowances. Tobacco and alcohol are especially cheap and a significant effort is put into stopping smuggling of cigarettes from Gibraltar to Spain. Note that the customs allowance is intended for one off trips. If you stay in La Línea and cross the border each day you are not meant to take a full duty free allowance each time. Officials are on the watch for local Spaniards doing exactly that.

Opening times

The shops on Main Street shut in the evening. Many are also closed on Sunday. The Post Office is closed on Saturday afternoons and Sundays. The Eroski supermarket at the frontier is open 8am-10pm every day.

Expect the Post Office, museum and WWII tunnels to be shut on bank holidays. For 2019 these are as follows:

2019 Bank holidays

Tuesday	1st January	New Year's Day
Monday	11th March	Commonwealth Day
Friday	19th April	Good Friday
Monday	22nd April	Easter Monday
Monday	29th April	Workers Memorial Day
Wednesday	1st May	May Day
Monday	27th May	Spring Bank Holiday
Monday	17th June	Queen's Birthday
Monday	26th August	Late Summer Bank Holiday
Tuesday	10th September	Gibraltar National Day
Wednesday	25th December	Christmas Day
Thursday	26th December	Boxing Day

Money

Gibraltar uses the British pound sterling, symbol £ and abbreviation GBP. The Gibraltar pound is exactly the same currency as the United Kingdom pound so no-one should charge you to change between them. Ignore incorrect internet articles telling you that the Gibraltar pound is actually a separate currency with abbreviation GIP. If you have a UK bank account then cash machine withdrawals from a UK bank, for example NatWest on Main Street, will not incur any charges. Similarly, electronic transactions are in pounds, the same as in the UK.

Confusion arises over the coins and notes. Gibraltar produces its own, a similar system to the local banknotes produced in Scotland and Northern Ireland. In Gibraltar you can use either Gibraltarian notes and coins or English ones. You will receive a mixture of the two in your change. At a cash machine you are likely to get Gibraltarian notes.

The Gibraltarian coins and notes are not accepted in UK shops. Although English (Bank of England) notes are accepted in Gibraltar, Irish and Scottish notes are not.

The best plan is to take English notes or collect Gibraltarian notes from a cash machine when you arrive. Plan your spend and keep track of your change to ensure you only have English notes and coins when you leave. If you are stuck with Gibraltarian money, either try and swap it in a shop or restaurant before leaving or you may be able to pay it into your UK bank account on your return. If you are not from the UK you will find Gibraltarian notes hard to exchange outside of Gibraltar.

Either convert them to another currency before leaving or swap them for English (marked "Bank of England") notes.

Most places in Gibraltar offer two prices, pounds and euros. The euro price is always much more expensive.

Accommodation

Many people visit Gibraltar on day trips. If you are visiting for longer you have two options. One is to stay in Gibraltar. An internet search will find you hotels.

The other is to stay in La Línea on the Spanish side of the border. If you are visiting as part of a longer holiday in Spain, this will save you carrying all your stuff through customs and into town. The accommodation in La Línea is cheap and it is only 7 minutes to walk from Avenida de España to the border. Crossing the border on foot only takes a few minutes under normal circumstances. Cafe Bar Eclen, beside the bus station, is a handy place to get breakfast.

Be very careful in La Línea, especially crossing the border at night. It has high crime and unemployment with a bad reputation amongst Spanish people in other parts of Spain. Don't plan on sight-seeing in La Línea. There is not much there and the line of fortifications that gave the town its name is long gone.

Food

Gibraltar has plenty of places to eat out. Casemates Square has numerous bars and restaurants with outside tables. Going through the archways to Market Place, you will find several more restaurants. There are a few pubs along Main Street which do food, including the Angry Friar, with its outside tables, and the Aragon, on Bell Lane. You will also find a few places to eat on the street called Irish Town. Past the far end of Main Street you will find the Mamma Mia Italian restaurant on Eliott's Way and the Trafalgar Pub, near the Trafalgar Cemetery.

If you are up in the nature reserve, there is a cafe and restaurant at the upper cable car station and also a cafe at St Michael's Cave.

For something fancier, Ocean Village has a huge range of restaurants with outdoor seats and a lovely setting. They are however busier and more expensive.

Spanish side of border and memorial to Spanish workers

La Línea bus station and nearby cafe

Gibraltar's entry road crosses the airport runway

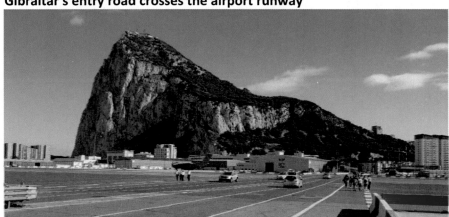

Section 3 - Getting there

Gibraltar's sovereignty is disputed by the Spanish government. Due to this, transport links from mainland Spain are poor. You have several options:

By boat:

Gibraltar is a popular port of call for Mediterranean cruise ships. These lucky people can step off their boat and move straight to the attractions described later.

There are also boat services to Morocco which may serve you, either as a short trip during your stay in Gibraltar itself or during a longer trip including North Africa. It is not possible to take a boat trip to Gibraltar from Malaga or other ports along the Spanish coast.

By air:

Amazingly, for a big rock on the coast, Gibraltar has its own airport. EasyJet have flights from the British airports of Manchester, Bristol and London Gatwick. British Airways offer flights from London Gatwick and London Heathrow. Royal Air Maroc provide flights from Casablanca and Tangiers in Morocco.

By car:

Driving from Malaga will only take about 1 hour 45 minutes. At the border with Gibraltar there is the possibility of long queues.

By train:

It is possible to take the train from Malaga to Algeciras. From Algeciras you must take the local bus to La Línea. The train takes 4 hours and only runs a few times a day with a change at Ronda. This makes the train a poor choice compared to the bus, unless you wish to break your journey at Ronda, a scenic town with a beautiful medieval bridge.

By bus:

From Malaga there are bus services every few hours to La Línea, the town on the Spanish side of Gibraltar's border. Faster and more frequent buses go from Malaga to Algeciras but from there you will need to take the local bus to La Línea. This takes 45 minutes so it is better to travel direct to La Línea if you can.

Buses leave Malaga bus station on Calle Mendivil, which is close to the Plaza de la Solidaridad and the Maria Zambrano railway station. You can buy tickets from the ticket desk in the bus station. It is worth buying tickets in advance since buses may be full, even outside of peak tourist season. Cost is 13 to 18 Euros each way, depending which bus you get. There are free toilets at both bus stations and also at Marbella, where the bus makes a brief stop.

The buses do not actually cross into Gibraltar. Instead they drop you at La Línea bus station, two minutes' walk from the border. Remember you will need your passport to cross. There are taxis on the La Línea side of the border crossing and sometimes outside of the bus station itself.

The bus timetable is on display at the bus station. Its unusual format is confusing if you do not speak Spanish. Rather than give a departure and arrival time, it only gives departure times. The journey duration is given for each route, allowing you to calculate your arrival time. Current timetable (May 2018) is as shown opposite.

As an example, the first bus on a Monday from Malaga to La Línea is at 06:45 and will arrive in La Línea 3 hours later - which you must work out for yourself is at 09:45. The first bus back leaves La Línea at 09:00 so (from the 3 hour journey time) will arrive in Malaga at 12:00.

The letters A, C and U after certain times are not important. It just means a different company supplies the bus. The stopping (Ruta) bus takes longest. Express (Directo and Semidirecto) are faster. The times in pink are for the nicer, but more expensive, "plus" coaches.

If you are staying in Spain and fancy a day trip, a faster, but slightly more expensive, option is to go on an organised day excursion from your hotel or direct from Malaga airport.

Malaga -- La Línea (Ruta) Duración del trayecto (Journey time) 3 hours
Fare 13.13 Euro
Monday to Saturday

Salida desde Malaga (leaves from Malaga)	6:45	11:30A	14:00	16:15	
Salida desde La Línea (leaves from La Línea)	9:00	10:30	16:30A	19:30	

Sundays and holidays

Leaves from Malaga	6:45	11:30A	14:00	16:15	19:15
Leaves from La Línea	9:00	10:30	16:30A	19:00	20:45

Malaga -- Algeciras (Ruta) Journey time 3 hours Fare 14.50 Euro
Monday to Saturday

Leaves Malaga	5:00	7:30	8:15	10:30U	11:30A	14:00	16:15	19:30
Leaves Algeciras	8:30	11:00	12:30	16:00A	17:00U	19:00	21:00	

Sundays and holidays

Leaves Malaga	5:00	7:30	8:30	10:30U	11:30A	14:00	15:30	16:30	19:30
Leaves Algeciras	8:30	11:00	12:00	16:00A	17:00U	18:30	21:00		

Malaga -- Algeciras (Directo) Journey time: 1 hour 45min Fare 14.96 Euro
Monday to Saturday (18.05 Euros for plus)

Leaves from Malaga	6:45	11:00A	13:00A	17:40	
Leaves from Algeciras	14:00A	15:00A	16:30	17:30	20:15

Sundays and holidays

Leaves from Malaga	6:45	11:00A	13:00A	17:30	
Leaves from Algeciras	14:00A	15:00A	16:30	17:30	19:30

Malaga -- Algeciras (Semidirecto) Journey time 2 hours 15 min
Fare 18.05 Euro
Monday to Saturday

Leaves Malaga	13:30C	14:00	15:30	19:25	20:00C	23:00	
Leaves Algeciras	06:45	07:30	09:00	09:30C	14:15	16:15C	22:15

Sundays and holidays

Leaves Malaga	13:30C	14:00	15:30	18:30	20:00C	23:00	
Leaves Algeciras	07:00	07:30	09:00	09:30	14:15	16:15C	22:15

Map 2 - Getting into Town

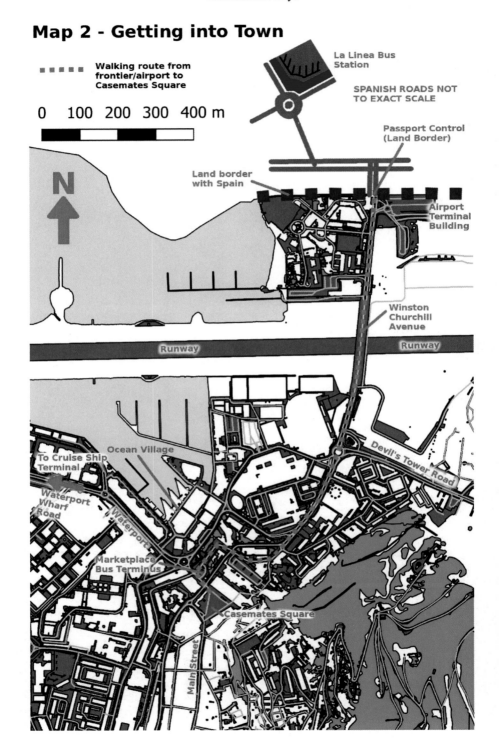

Walking route from frontier/airport to Casemates Square

0   100   200   300   400 m

La Linea Bus Station

SPANISH ROADS NOT TO EXACT SCALE

Passport Control (Land Border)

Land border with Spain

N

Airport Terminal Building

Winston Churchill Avenue

Runway   Runway

Ocean Village

Devil's Tower Road

To Cruise Ship Terminal

Waterport Wharf Road

Waterport

Marketplace Bus Terminus

Casemates Square

Main Street

Orientation on Arrival

By bus

Walk into the bus station building and out of the other side. On this side the building curves around a roundabout. You will see the Rock of Gibraltar and a few flags marking the crossing point. Walk towards the Rock and cross the busy road. The customs post is obvious with signs above the car lanes. The pedestrian route is less obvious and is situated in the white buildings to the sides of the car lanes. To enter Gibraltar walk into the building on the right hand side of the car lanes.

After going through Spanish and British passport control you enter a small corridor with historic photos of Gibraltar. A stall will try and sell you taxi based Rock Tours. On leaving this building you will find yourself on Winston Churchill Avenue, the only road into Gibraltar. The Rock is in front of you and the airport terminal building is across the road, to your left.

The customs point for leaving Gibraltar is on the opposite side of the road so on returning to Spain you will also keep to the right of the car lanes. The return route for pedestrians is poorly marked and can vary depending on what checks are taking place. Keep to the right of the car lanes, close to the road. The doorway doesn't look much but you will see a passport control sign when you are right up to it.

By air

On leaving the terminal building there is a taxi rank in the airport carpark. Alternatively walk across Winston Churchill Avenue and follow the instructions below.

Getting from the border into town

Whether crossing the border on foot or arriving by air you will end up at the same place, the end of Winston Churchill Avenue. A small kiosk here sells refreshments.

There is a taxi rank here. The drivers will sell you tickets for Rock Tours. Note that the per person price assumes you will wait for other customers so they have a full cab. Be prepared to wait and make sure you are not paying for any empty spaces. You might have trouble getting a taxi for an ordinary journey as the tours are more profitable. You could also try the taxi rank across the road at the airport terminal.

Buses into town leave from a stop on Winston Churchill Avenue, just after the taxis. On the return trip they drop you in the airport carpark. Bus 5 takes you to Market Place, beside Casemates Square, the perfect place to start a leisurely wander of Gibraltar's Main Street or sit outside with a beer or pub meal. The number 10 does not go to Market Place but is useful if you plan to cut out Main Street and head straight for Trafalgar Cemetery and the cable car.

Buy your bus ticket on board from the driver or from the conductor who often stands beside the stop. Just past the bus stop (and near enough to visit, even if you plan on getting the bus) is the huge Eroski supermarket. This is a good place to stock up on water and snacks as you enter Gibraltar or buy duty free liquor on the way out.

If you prefer to walk, it will take about 20 minutes to reach Casemates Square from the border. Follow the route (shown as a pink dotted line) on page 18.

The road and footpath to Gibraltar cross the runway of the airport. Should a plane wish to use the runway, guards close the pedestrian path first, then the road. Finally a road sweeper vehicle comes out to give the multi-use section a quick clean. The whole thing takes about 15 minutes so don't be concerned if you get caught waiting for it. The process is interesting to watch and worth experiencing if you have time.

By cruise ship

From the cruise terminal it will also take about 20 minutes to walk to Casemates Square. A shuttlebus might be available. You can also get a taxi tour from the cruise port. The ordinary buses stop on Waterport and Europort Roads but do not go right to the cruise terminal.

By car

Vehicles drive on the right, the same as Spain. Note that there are no fees to cross the border. Conmen in uniforms sometimes approach queueing traffic to try and charge one. There are several large carparks. Grand Parade carpark is beside the cable car station.

Section 4 - Suggested Itineraries

Since this book is called Gibraltar in 2 days, it is assumed you are in a hurry. Gibraltar is a small place but you still won't be able to see everything. The exact choice will depend on your interests and the length of your stay but here are some suggested plans to get the most out of your visit.

Less than a full day

Perhaps you are on a day trip from Malaga or a cruise. You arrive mid-morning and must leave early evening.

For such a short visit you need to plan carefully. It would be easy to waste the morning wandering around the town centre or find yourself somewhere up on the Rock, an hour's walk from Main Street, worrying about catching your bus.

A good option would be to visit the nature reserve first. Be sure to see the Great Siege Tunnels and the monkeys, at either Apes' Den or the upper cable car station. After exploring the nature reserve you can finish with a quick walk along Main Street and get a beer in the Angry Friar (on Main Street) or relax in Casemates Square. You might want to take food and drink (especially water) with you. There are restaurants at the top cable car station and St Michael's Cave.

If you don't spend too long on the Rock you might have time to visit the museum. If you like walking, however, you may prefer to stay in the nature reserve longer, visiting the Moorish Castle, City Under Siege, Great Siege Tunnels, St Michael's Cave, the Skywalk and the Windsor Bridge. Starting at Moorish Castle and leaving via the Jews' Gate entrance then walking back along Main Street would give a nice circular route but you would need to be organised to fit it all in.

Such a route would involve about 3 to 3½ hours of walking (including the walk back along Main Street) plus 1 to 2 hours inside the attractions. You are unlikely to have time for the Mediterranean steps or O'Hara's Battery.

You might want to save time by taking the taxi based Rock Tour, the cable car or by using the buses, at least for some of your journey. Make sure you have time to get back. From Jews' Gate to Casemates Square is 45 minutes' walk. If you are crossing the frontier, remember you could potentially be delayed by planes using the runway or if passport control takes longer than the normal few minutes.

A full day

As above, your priority should be the Upper Rock. With less rush in the evening you can afford to stay on the Rock until closing time at 19:15 or even be wandering down after this. Since the shops and museum shut by 18:00, you may be better having a look at these in the morning. That way you can relax for as long as you like on the Rock's paths and look forward to a meal and a well-earned beer when you get down

Should your day trip include arrival the night before, it is worth exploring, even if this means crossing from La Línea for just a few hours. The border crossing does not normally take long and is open 24 hours a day.

Two days

Two days will give you a good taste of Gibraltar. You still won't see everything.

Unless the weather is bad I suggest you spend the first day on the Upper Rock. Try and head up reasonably early to spend a full day walking the scenic routes. Either take some food with you or buy a snack at the cafes beside the top cable car station or St Michael's Cave. Be sure to take plenty of water. Once you have made the steep climb up from the town you will certainly not want to go back down. It will probably be quite late when you come down but you can have a walk along Main Street and get some food and a drink, even though the shops and museum will be shut.

On your second day you can explore the town centre and museum. You can call in at the tourist information office and check out other historical items in the centre. While passing through Casemates Square be sure to see the free glassmaking exhibition, walk through the Landport gate and go up to the balcony overlooking the square, with its art and craft shops.

Wander along Main Street to the Trafalgar cemetery and through Irish Town. For a slightly more upmarket meal or drink, walk down to Ocean Village although the outside tables here can be busier than Casemates Square.

At some point during your visit, it is worth walking along Winston Churchill Avenue to see the runway, particularly if you can catch a plane taking off or landing.

If you are feeling energetic you might be able to squeeze in another more distant attraction. The Botanic Gardens are pleasant if you want a gentle walk. If you get the bus you could visit Europa Point or go to Rosia Bay and see the 100 ton gun. You could also go back up to the nature reserve if you enjoyed the walking or didn't see everything you wanted to.

More than two days

With more time you have the luxury of spreading your trip out. I'd still recommend going to the Upper Rock sooner rather than later but there is no need to go your first day. You might want to make several visits and check out smaller attractions up there, for example all of the gun batteries and the Mediterranean steps.

You could afford to spend your first day wandering the town centre or having a relaxing drink in the bars of Casemates Square. In this case the museum and tourist information office, both located half way along Main Street, would be good things to visit on your first day.

You should easily fit in trips to items like the 100 ton gun and could head round to the beaches on the other side of the Rock. Nowhere in Gibraltar is very far. For example, Europa point to Market Place (beside Casemates Square) is only 22 minutes by bus.

Finally, with plenty of time to see everything on the Rock you are interested in, it is realistic to consider other activities. You could take a boat trip for example. I do not recommend crossing into Spain. The town of La Línea across the border has nothing to recommend a visit.

Map 3 - Upper Rock (north)

Princess Anne's Battery

Great Siege Tunnels

Casemates Square

Princess Caroline's Battery

World War II Tunnels

Moorish Castle and Entrance

Governor's Battery

Main Street

City Under Siege

Bell Lane

Queen's Road

Signal Station Road

Devil's Gap Battery

Inglis Way

Queen's Road

Trafalgar Cemetery

N

Old Queen's Road

Queen's Road

Cable Car Station (Top)

Cable Car Bottom Station

Apes' Den

Charles V Wall (Top of wall forms a stepped path)

↓ page 26

Section 5 - List of Attractions

Upper Rock Nature Reserve

The Upper Rock Nature Reserve is the best part of Gibraltar, especially if you enjoy walking. It is worth prioritising a trip up here and not wasting too much time in the town. The paths can be steep.

Access to the Upper Rock is possible in four ways:

- **At Jews' Gate**, 30 minutes' walk uphill from Trafalgar Cemetery
- **At the Moorish Castle**, a steep walk up many steps from the Casemates Square end of Main Street (or take the No. 1 bus)
- **By cable car** from Grand Parade, near Trafalgar Cemetery
- **By taxi**, using the Rock Tours

Entry to the nature reserve requires a ticket

- **5 pounds (Walker ticket)** - Includes Skywalk, Windsor Bridge and Mediterranean Steps. You can also visit O'Hara's battery and see the monkeys in the Apes' Den.
- **12 pounds (Walking plus attractions)** Includes St Michael's Cave, Great Siege Tunnels, City Under Siege Exhibition and Moorish castle
- **20 pounds** - all attractions plus Second World War Tunnels

The cable car costs £13.50 single and £15.50 return. To this must be added one of the nature reserve tickets. Children (£6.50 return), students and senior citizens, 65 and over, get discounts. The middle cable car station (next to the Apes' Den) is only open during winter.

Nature reserve tickets last one day but it is worth explaining your plans to the ticket seller if you are visiting for more than one day. If you are lucky they might extend it. If you only buy the 12 pound ticket and later decide to see the World War II Tunnels you can pay the 8 pounds extra to upgrade your ticket.

The nature reserve itself is open from 09:30 to 19:15 with last entry to the attractions at 18:45. In winter (November to March) it is open 09:00-18:15 with last entry at 17:45. Don't worry too much about being locked in. After closing time the post at Jews' Gate is deserted

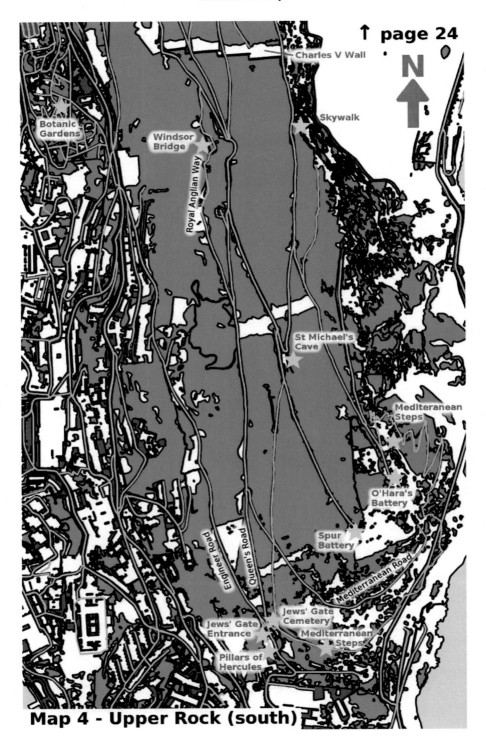

↑ page 24

N

Charles V Wall

Skywalk

Botanic Gardens

Windsor Bridge

Royal Anglian Way

St Michael's Cave

Mediteranean Steps

O'Hara's Battery

Engineer Road

Queen's Road

Spur Battery

Mediterranean Road

Jews' Gate Cemetery

Jews' Gate Entrance

Mediterranean Steps

Pillars of Hercules

Map 4 - Upper Rock (south)

but you can still walk past. The metal gates further downhill are not locked until 22:00.

Look at the map and choose your entry point and route. It would be hard to fit everything into one trip but don't miss the Great Siege Tunnels and the monkeys at either Apes' Den or the cable car station.

If you are walking to the Moorish Castle entrance from Main Street, take Bell Lane. At the end of this street continue uphill along steep streets and stairs. At the top you turn left to reach the Moorish Castle and the nature reserve entrance. The route is fairly obvious. You could also take Engineer Lane (not to be confused with Engineer Road) but the sign for this is harder to see than the one for Bell Lane.

If you are walking to the Jews' Gate entrance, take Europa Road past the Botanic Gardens. The road to the Upper Rock branches off to the left and is indicated with a huge sign some distance before the turning. It will take you 30 minutes to walk from Trafalgar Cemetery to Jews' Gate.

If you wish to save time and uphill walking you should consider the bus. Bus number 1 stops near the Moorish Castle and several buses stop at the Rock Hotel and Old Casino on Europa Road near the Botanic Gardens. Note that it is still over 20 minutes' walk from Europa Road to the Jews' Gate entrance.

If you are travelling from the frontier, bus 10 allows you to go direct from the frontier to Boyd Street, near Grand Parade. From this stop, either walk through the underpass to Grand Parade and the cable car station or head up Europa Road past the Botanic Gardens and then take the road to Jews' Gate.

Private cars are not allowed on the Upper Rock. There is a huge car park at Grand Parade

Your nature reserve entry includes a leaflet with a free map. This suggests routes for nature lovers, history buffs, thrill seekers and a monkey trail. These routes are very good but can be hard to follow since there are many branches in the paths which are not shown. It is worth using the maps in this book to complement the suggested routes.

Moorish Castle

Moorish Castle

This square tower, called The Tower of Homage, was mostly constructed by the Moors in the 14th century. The foundations date to an earlier fortress built around 1160. One face of the tower shows damage from shot, probably from an early siege that occurred in 1333.

Inside are stairs down to the basement and up to the rooftop but there are only a few rooms to visit. There is a small garden with a seat but apart from that you are unlikely to spend more than 20 minutes here.

World War II tunnels

Continuing up the Rock from the Moorish Castle, you will reach the entrance to the World War II tunnels. During the war the tunnel network was increased to 34 miles. Unlike the older Great Siege Tunnels, which are included in the £12 nature reserve ticket, entry to the WWII tunnels requires you to pay an extra £8. You must also book a guided tour, either at the tourist information office or by phoning **+350 200 45000, +350 200 71643** or **+350 200 71648** Mon-Fri or emailing **ur&beaches@gibraltar.gov.gi**

Entrance to World War II Tunnels

The tours run Mon-Fri, 0930-1700 and last about 30-40 minutes. Note that the WWII tunnels are closed on bank holidays. Since the WWII tunnels are operated by a different company to the Great Siege Tunnels and other attractions, information from staff at the main ticket gates can sometimes be wrong. If the WWII tunnels are an important part of your visit you should book your tour well ahead to be certain they are open and that you can get a place.

If you miss the WWII tunnels, the Great Siege Tunnels are an impressive and cheaper alternative and also include some information about the Rock's defences during World War II.

City Under Siege

This is a small, outdoor exhibition, between the WWII tunnels and Princess Caroline's Battery.

It includes ruined buildings which illustrate the state of the city after the Great Siege. Dioramas and posters describe the harsh conditions for those who lived through it. There are interesting facts, for example the paving slabs were lifted and the streets ploughed so cannonballs would embed themselves harmlessly in the earth rather than ricocheting around.

During the Great Siege, the nearby lime kiln was used to heat cannonballs red hot. They were then carried in wheelbarrows filled with sand to be fired at the attacking French and Spanish.

Allow about 15 minutes for your visit.

City Under Siege Exhibition

Princess Caroline's battery

Continuing up the Rock from the City Under Siege exhibition, you will come to a large concrete gun emplacement. The gun itself is no longer here and the concrete structure has been painted green. It is a pleasant place to sit and take a break, with excellent views of the airport runway and the Spanish border if you wish to take photographs. There is sometimes an ice cream van.

The buildings immediately behind the green concrete area contain a Military Heritage Centre. Part submerged, they are easy to miss if you are not looking for them.

Free toilets are located nearby on the path towards the Great Siege Tunnels.

Great Siege Tunnels

This exhibit dates from Gibraltar's Great Siege of 1779 to 1782. During this siege, Spanish troops tried to reclaim Gibraltar. The shape of the Rock created an area where attackers were partially shielded from the British defenders' cannon. To solve this a tunnel was dug towards a rocky outcrop known as The Notch.

View of runway and La Línea from Princess Caroline's Battery

The original aim was to build an access path so a cannon could be mounted on top of The Notch and cover the blind spot. During tunnelling it was realised a better idea was to mount cannon within the Rock itself, firing out through small windows.

Cannon were placed along the tunnel. After the end of the siege the tunnel was continued and eventually reached the original target of The Notch. Instead of mounting a gun on top, this was hollowed out into the huge St George's Hall, a spacious cavern holding seven cannon.

In 1785 the tunnel was extended to the other side of the Rock to reach the previously inaccessible Holyland ledge. This was used as a machine gun post during the Second World War.

Displays explain the progress and changes in the tunneller's plans and describe important battles during the Great Siege. Well-designed posters give interesting pieces of historical information. For example, during the Great Siege, shot that embedded itself in the soft earth caused less damage. Captain Mercier experimented with fuses to make the shells explode before hitting the ground. After the siege his ideas were further developed by Colonel Shrapnel, who gave the shell fragments his name.

Along with the monkeys, the Great Siege Tunnels are one of the highlights of the Upper Rock and should not be missed. If possible allow 45 minutes to 1 hour for your visit and take time to read the posters explaining the tunnels' history. The tunnels are well-lit and airy, especially the parts before the Holyland Tunnel.

Cannon inside the Great Siege Tunnels

Holyland Tunnel and Holyland Ledge

Monkeys sunbathing at Apes' Den

Apes' Den

This is an outdoor area where the apes congregate, although they can be found throughout the nature reserve and even on the roads approaching it. At several points, including this den, the wardens put out food so there is an extra incentive for the little creatures to hang out.

It is strictly forbidden to feed the monkeys. Not only is it bad for the monkeys, it encourages them to see people as a food source which results in them harassing and possibly biting the tourists.

This policy appears to have been successful since the apes completely ignore people. When you want one to look round for a photograph it is as though you are not there. Their indifference to humans does not extend to vehicles. You will probably see them playing on parked and even moving cars in the reserve.

You will have no problem seeing many apes and get very close. Don't get too close as they are lightning fast when they want to move. Ensure they don't bite you or steal your camera. The baby apes are the most active. After the hard climb you could easily spend much time sitting in the sun, watching the apes at play, while admiring the fantastic view.

Charles V Wall

Charles V Wall

The lower part of this wall (which houses the Southport and Referendum gates) was started in 1552 to protect the town after an earlier pirate attack. It was later extended from the Apes' Den area to the top of the Rock. Steps on the top form a long staircase, allowing you to walk from the Apes' Den to the top cable car station. The photo shows about a quarter of the climb. You will be exhausted when you reach the top.

The upper cable car station is a popular area for monkeys

Cable Car Station

This is your first stop if you arrive by cable car and one of the highest points if you are walking. Inside are a cafe, restaurant and a small display about the monkeys. The cartoons depicting the hazards of feeding the monkeys are amusing and deserve a more prominent position.

Boards give interesting explanations of monkey behaviour. For example, the Round Mouthed Threat is a pouting face the monkeys pull when annoyed. It translates roughly as "stop annoying me or something bad will happen." Running away too quickly from an angry monkey is also bad. It signals complete surrender which encourages the monkey to attack.

Be careful that the monkeys do not steal your things, especially bags, which they hope will contain food.

Sky Walk

If you don't mind heights, this glass floored platform lets you walk out from the cliff for an exhilarating view. It is 340m above sea level with a view in all directions to let you see Gibraltar and its surroundings.

The Windsor Bridge

Windsor Bridge

This suspension bridge allows walkers on the Royal Anglian Way footpath to cut across a gulley on a slightly wobbly bridge with a huge drop beneath their feet. If you don't like crossing scary bridges with just a couple of inches of wood between you and a 50 metre drop, the path continues along on solid ground. You can therefore bypass the bridge in almost the same time it takes your thrill seeking friends to cross it.

O'Hara's Battery

Although you might have thought the cable car station was higher, this gun battery marks the highest point in Gibraltar. Two huge guns are mounted here, covering the Strait of Gibraltar. As you are near the south of the Rock you also have a good view towards the mountains of Morocco across the Mediterranean.

O'Hara's battery is at one end of the Mediterranean Steps path which runs from here to Jews' Gate.

Gun at O'Hara's Battery

St Michael's Cave

This large cavern is filled with stalagmites, stalactites and almost every other related type of rock formation.

On entering the cave you find yourself in a large cavern. Tiered steps are built into the floor to provide an auditorium. It is a large space so no need to worry about crawling through narrow tunnels. The rock formations are illuminated with coloured lights.

A huge stalagmite on the floor collapsed thousands of years ago. The end of this has been cut and polished and the cut face resembles agate. Coloured bands show how rainfall levels have varied over the years and also the last two ice ages.

St Michael's Cave

Wandering away from the main cavern you can see other parts of the cave, including an underground lake and some places without the coloured lights.

The cave was prepared as a military hospital and used for police and fire training so has not been well cared for. Some of it is only visible because the main cave was widened with explosives.

St Michael's Cave is well worth seeing but you will not need to spend a long time here. Allow about 20 minutes.

At the entrance are cafe facilities, a gift shop and free toilets. You will also find many monkeys in this area.

Spur Battery

Another gun emplacement. The gun has now been removed and is in the Imperial War Museum in England.

Jews' Gate Cemetery

The Jews were resented in Spain for having co-operated with the Moors. Under the Treaty of Utrecht the British were not officially allowed to permit them to live in Gibraltar. The Jews also did not want their cemetery to overlook Spain, having been persecuted there by the Spanish Inquisition.

For these reasons this Jewish Cemetery was built at the south end of Gibraltar.

The Pillars of Hercules Monument

Pillars of Hercules

Beside the Jews' Gate entrance to the Upper Rock is the Pillars of Hercules monument. This commemorates Gibraltar's place in ancient history as Mount Calpe, one of two pillars separated by the Strait of Gibraltar. These pillars marked the gateway at the end of the Mediterranean to the unknown dangers of the Atlantic Ocean. You may wish to get your photo taken beside it but beyond that it is just a monument and nothing special to see.

Mediterranean Steps

This steep, twisting path provides a scenic route between the Jews' Gate Cemetery and O'Hara's battery. It consists of narrow paths and steps cut into the cliff face.

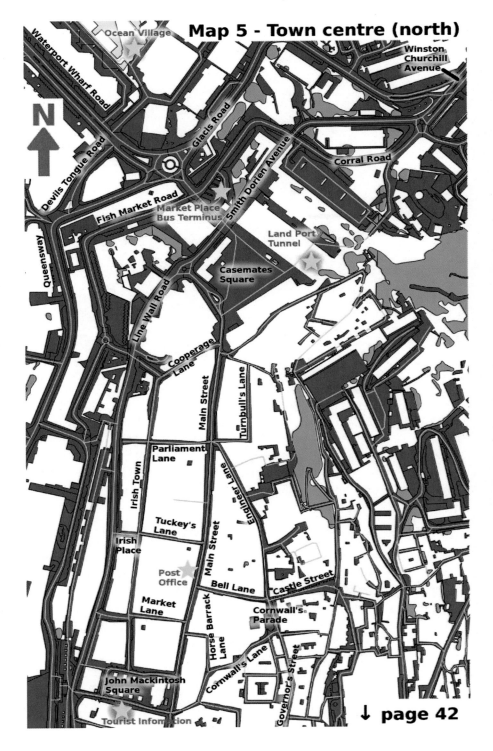

Map 5 - Town centre (north)

↓ page 42

Around Main Street

Gibraltar's main bus terminus is the Market Place bus stop. Walking from the cruise ship terminal, airport or Spanish border, this is also your entry point to the city centre. Beside Market Place is Casemates Square. This large open area, full of pubs and restaurants, is a major landmark for you to get your bearings.

At the far corner of this square is Main Street. This is the town's high street and runs the full length of the city centre, from Casemates Square in the north to the Southport Gates, beside the Trafalgar Cemetery.

Walking south along Main Street, away from Casemates, the Rock of Gibraltar is on your left. The streets rise steeply on this side and give access to the nature reserve by the Moorish Castle entrance. To the right, running parallel to Main Street is the street called Irish Town.

Casemates Square viewed from the balcony on the north-east side

Casemates Square

From the Market Place bus terminus, enter Casemates Square through the Grand Casemates Gates in the city wall. The square itself has a huge amount of outdoor seating, should you wish to enjoy a drink or

↑ page 40

Map 6 - Town centre (south)

↓ page 44

Glass Museum and Landport Gate

meal from the many restaurants. Often there is a temporary stage with music.

On the left side as you enter is the glass blowing museum. Glass was Gibraltar's only manufacturing industry and the museum is worth a look although it will not take long.

Past the glass blowing museum you can enter a hallway and staircase that give you access to the upper balcony with a nice view across the square and access to the small craft shops on the upper floor. There are also some nice free toilets.

Continuing to the eastern corner, beside the Lord Nelson pub, is the Landport tunnel. Go through this tunnel to see the Landport gate. This was once the only access to the city other than by boat.

At the southern corner of the square is the start of Main Street. There is a shopping mall on the corner. This contains a small branch of the Eroski supermarket if you need to stock up on snacks or water.

Main Street

Main Street is a long, block paved street, mostly restricted to pedestrians. The shops are aimed at tourists and not very interesting. It will take at least 15 minutes to walk the length of Main Street, excluding any time looking at the shops.

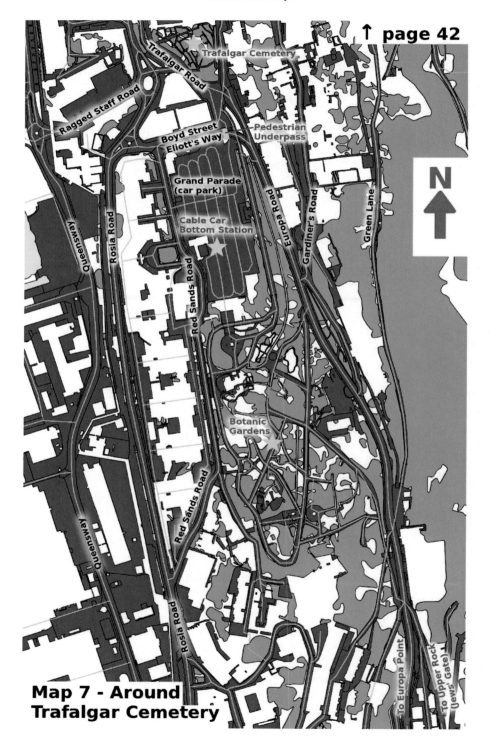

↑ page 42

Map 7 - Around
Trafalgar Cemetery

The Post Office on Main Street

You can get spirits and cigarettes for amazing prices, even compared to Spain. Shops also push perfume and to a lesser extent, electrical goods. The perfume is much cheaper that the UK but not as big a bargain as the alcohol and tobacco. For electrical goods there is not a lot of choice and you should check UK prices to be sure you are really saving anything.

Just after leaving Casemates Square, the NatWest bank on the left has a cash machine. There is also one further along on the right, at Jyst Bank, just before the Post Office, and another at the far end, at the Gibraltar International Bank, near the Southport Gates.

About a quarter of the way along you will see the Post Office with a double size red post box in the doorway. The post boxes were installed bearing the initial of the reigning monarch and Main Street claims to have a red post box from every British monarch since post boxes were introduced.

Post Office hours: Mon-Thur 1000-1300, 1330-1615; Fri 1000-1300, 1330-1600; Sat 1000-1300.

The Post Office is closed Sundays and bank holidays. Many shops will sell stamps with postcards but check they have them before you buy your cards. Some will only sell stamps if you also buy a postcard.

The Angry Friar, part way along Main Street, is a good place for pub food with lots of outdoor, marble topped tables.

Tourist Information

This is located on a side street on John Mackintosh Square, half way along Main Street.

Opening hours: Mon-Fri 09:00-16:30, Sat 09:30-15:30, Sun & bank holidays 10:00-1300

Telephone: (+350) 200 45000 **email:** information@tourism.gov.gi

There is also an office at the frontier, which opens weekdays only, and one at the cruise terminal, which only opens when a ship is in port.

Cathedral of St Mary the Crowned

This is the Roman Catholic cathedral and is built on the site of an earlier mosque.

Cathedral of the Holy Trinity

This Anglican cathedral is located on Cathedral Square and built in the style of Moorish architecture.

Irish Town

Irish Town is a street which runs parallel to Main Street. It was named after two ships carrying Irish woman immigrants who were encouraged to move to Gibraltar. It was hoped that this would improve morale and discipline of the soldiers who were bored in the garrison town and had little to do but drink. The street was completely destroyed by enemy cannon during the Great Siege. In the 19th century it became a wealthy area inhabited by merchants.

There are a few cafes and restaurants on this street. If you wish to explore its history more fully, the tourist information office have a leaflet explaining the history of each building.

Gibraltar Museum

The Gibraltar museum is just off Main Street on Bomb House Lane, not far from the tourist information office - see the black signposts on Main Street. The museum's basement is a 14th Century Moorish baths. Displays illustrate both the natural history and archaeology of Gibraltar and its more recent social and military history.

It is open Mon-Fri 1000-1800; Sat 1000-1400; closed Sundays and bank holidays. Entry is £5.

Around Trafalgar Cemetery

At the southern end of Main Street are the Southport Gates which pass through the lower end of the Charles V Wall. The wider arch next to them is the Referendum Gate, named when Gibraltar voted to remain British in 1967. Passing south through the gates you will find the Trafalgar Cemetery. To the west are the Ragged Staff Gates. Should you wish to save walking along Main Street, the No. 10 bus will take you directly here (Boyd Street stop) from the airport and Spanish border.

While not comparable to Casemates Square, there are a few restaurants and pubs in this area. Try the Trafalgar pub, near Trafalgar Cemetery, or Mamma Mia Italian restaurant on Eliott's Way.

Heading past the cemetery, along Europa Road, you will find the Botanic Gardens. Near the gardens you can take the No. 2 bus to Europa Point or take the side road up to Jews' Gate.

Walking beneath Eliott's Way through an underpass you will find a large carpark called Grand Parade. This contains the cable car bottom station.

Underpass to Grand Parade carpark and cable car lower station

Trafalgar Cemetery

This green, leafy cemetery is named after Admiral Nelson's victory in the sea battle of 1805. Those who died in the fighting were buried at sea but the cemetery contains the graves of two sailors who were injured in the fighting and later died of their wounds.

Botanic Gardens

Botanic Gardens

The Botanic Gardens consist of a pleasant park. Paths are lined with trees, shrubs and small cacti. While worth a visit, it is not a must see destination if you are short of time. It is open every day 0800-2100 (or sunset if earlier). Entry to the gardens is free. The gardens contain several free toilets.

Within the gardens is a small zoo, the Alameda Wildlife Conservation Park. This houses an assortment of small animals from endangered species which have been rescued. It costs £5 and is open every day 1000-1645 except some bank holidays.

In addition to the entrance on Europa Road, the Botanic Gardens have a gate leading directly to the Grand Parade carpark, which houses the lower cable car station.

Grand Parade carpark and lower cable car station

Other attractions

100 ton gun

At Rosia Bay you can see the 100 ton gun. Four were manufactured for Malta and Gibraltar, the only other surviving one is in Malta. Rosia Bay was also the place that Nelson's ship Victory was towed to for temporary repairs after the battle of Trafalgar.

Opening hours: 09:30-18:45, every day. Cost £3 or included in price of the Upper Rock Nature Reserve ticket.

Beaches

Gibraltar has a number of beaches. The largest is Eastern Beach, near the airport, which gets all day sunshine. Catalan Bay is popular but falls in the shadow of the Rock as the sun sets. Next to it is Sandy Bay, a smaller beach which has recently been refurbished with sand imported from the Sahara.

Europa Point

Europa Point

At the most southern tip of Gibraltar is Europa Point. It is nearly the most southerly point in Europe, narrowly losing out to nearby coastline on the Algeciras side the bay. It is easily accessible by the No.2 bus - about 8 minutes from the Rock Hotel stop beside the Botanic Gardens or 22 minutes from the Market Place terminus next to Casemates Square.

There is a lighthouse and a large mosque and also a gun battery. A memorial commemorates General Sikorski, the Polish prime minister in exile, who was killed in a plane crash near here in 1943.

There is a cafeteria with a huge children's playground. You can also enjoy walks along the promenade. While a pleasant place to visit on a sunny day, it is more of a landmark than a place to explore.

Ocean Village

Ocean Village

Easily reached by bus or on foot from Casemates Square or the frontier, Ocean Village is a marina surrounded by restaurants and bars. Wide paths allow you to wander around and most of the bars have outside seating. They are more upmarket than the ones in Casemates Square and the outside tables tend to be busier.

There are two casinos here. Despite Gibraltar's status as a centre for online gambling, they do not offer much in the way of poker.

To the north of the Ocean Village bar area, further along Marina Bay, it is possible to book short dolphin watching cruises and other boat trips.

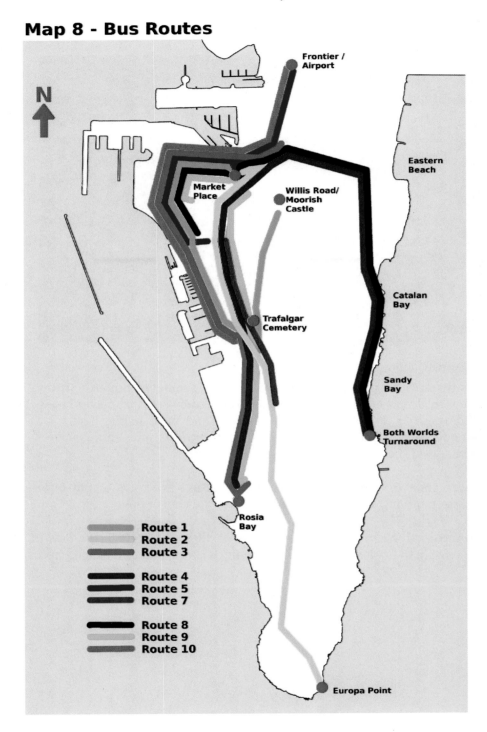

Map 8 - Bus Routes

N

Frontier / Airport

Eastern Beach

Market Place

Willis Road/ Moorish Castle

Catalan Bay

Trafalgar Cemetery

Sandy Bay

Both Worlds Turnaround

Rosia Bay

Europa Point

Route 1
Route 2
Route 3

Route 4
Route 5
Route 7

Route 8
Route 9
Route 10

Section 6 - Buses in Gibraltar

There are two bus companies in Gibraltar:

- **Calypso Transport Ltd (Citibus)** - Operates route 5 and route 10 - the only buses that go to the airport/Spanish border
- **Gibraltar Bus Company Ltd** - Operates all other buses

Hoppa tickets give one day's unlimited travel but only for the bus routes of the company issuing the ticket. The last buses set off at 21:00. On Fridays and Saturdays there is a very limited night bus service.

Adult Prices (Discounts for children and Senior Citizens)

	Calypso Citibus (Routes 5 & 10)	Gibraltar Bus Co. (Other routes)
Single	£1.30	£1.80
Return	£2.00	--
Hoppa	£3.00	£2.50
10 trip ticket	£8.00	--

The Gibraltar Bus Company offers free travel to permanent residents of Gibraltar and those with British M.O.D identity cards.

The Gibraltar Bus Company have a tracking system on their website (**www.gibraltarbuscompany.gi/site**) which shows the location of their buses in real time. Unfortunately the lists of stops on the website, bus tracker and on the posters at the stops themselves are all slightly different. The following pages list the stops based on the most up to date which, at the time of printing, is the posters. Be aware though that the routes may change slightly. Although the bus stops display details of route 6, this route is no-longer in operation.

The posters in the bus stops show every bus. You need to look at the sign beside the stops to find out which routes actually stop there. This is further complicated by the fact none of the stops display their names. There is also no indication if the route 5 or route 10 buses stop there because these belong to a rival company. The map on page 52 shows a rough outline of each route. The stops are listed on pages 54 and 55. Note that the buses stop in slightly different places on the inbound and outbound parts of their route.

Route 1		Route 2	
↓ Outbound	↑ Inbound	↓ Outbound	↑ Inbound
Willis Road Terminus	Willis Road Terminus	Market Place	Market Place
	Moorish Castle estate	Glacis Kiosk	Fish Market Steps
	Artillery Arms	Orange Bastion	
Arengo's Palace	Arengo's Palace	British War Memorial	NatWest Bank
Flat Bastion Road		Cathedral Square	Convent Place
Morello's Ramp (Astoria)		Referendum Gates	
Lower Flat Bastion Road		Eliott's Way	Trafalgar Cemetery
Gardiner's Road	Sacred Heart Church	Rock Hotel	
Trafalgar Cemetery (top)	Wilson's Ramp	Old Casino	
Queensway Quay (East)	Queensway Quay	Shorthorn Farm	Shorthorn Farm
Commonwealth Park	King's Wharf	Brympton	Mount Pleasant
Mid-Harbour Estate	Mid-Harbour Estate	Garrison Gym	Garrison Gym
Bishop Canilla House	Europort Building 8	North Gorge	North Gorge
St Bernard's Hospital	St Bernard's Hospital	Buena Vista	Buena Vista
Edinburgh House	Reclamation Road	Eliott's Battery	
Reclamation Road	Edinburgh House	Mosque	Mosque
Varyl Begg Estate		Europa Point	Europa Point
Sir William Jackson Grove			
Waterport Road			
Marketplace Terminus	Marketplace Terminus		

Route 3		Route 4	
↓ Outbound	↑ Inbound	↓ Outbound	↑ Inbound
South Pavilion Steps	South Pavilion Steps	Both Worlds (turnaround)	Both Worlds (turnaround)
St Joseph's School	St Joseph's School	Both Worlds	
Rosia Plaza		Black Strap Cove	
Rosia		Caleta Hotel	William's Way
New Mole House	Schomberg	Catalan Bay	
Cumberland	Shorthorn Farm	Eastern Beach	Eastern Beach
Jumper's Building	Old Casino	St Theresa's Church	
Victoria House	Rock Hotel	Park & Ride Garage	St Theresa's Church
Trafalgar Cemetery (top)	Eliott's Way	Referendum House	Faulknor House
Queensway Quay (East)	Queensway Quay	Constitution House	Notre Dame School
Commonwealth Park	King's Wharf	Market Place	Glacis Kiosk
Mid-Harbour Estate	Mid-Harbour Estate	Glacis Kiosk	Market Place
Bishop Canilla House	Europort Building 8	Orange Bastion	Fish Market Steps
St Bernard's Hospital	St Bernard's Hospital	British War Memorial	NatWest Bank
Varyl Begg Estate		Cathedral Square	Convent Place
Sir William Jackson Grove	GASA Swimming Pool	Referendum Gates	Trafalgar Cemetery
Waterport Road	Albert Risso House	Alameda House	Victoria House
Glacis Kiosk	Ocean Village	Governor's Meadow House	Jumper's Building
Notre Dame School	Constitution House	Jumper's Building	Cumberland
Referendum House Terminus	Referendum House Terminus	New Harbours	New Mole House
		South Gate	St Joseph's School
		Rosia Plaza	South Pavilion Steps
		Rosia Terminus	Rosia Terminus

Route 5

↓ Inward	↑ Outward
Frontier/Airport	Frontier/Airport
Glacis Estate	Notre Dame School/ Winston Churchill Ave
Marina Bay/ Casino/Dolphin trips	Glacis Junction
Market Place Term.	Market Place Term.
Ocean Village/ Watergardens	Watergardens
Waterport/ Port/ Albert Risso House	Sir William Jackson Grove
GASA swimming pool	
Europort/ Hospital/ McDonald's/ Morrisons superstore	Varyl Begg Estate/ Morrisons superstore
Queensway	
City Centre/ Main Street	

Route 8

↓ Outbound	↑ Inbound
Both Worlds (Turnaround)	Both Worlds (Turnaround)
Both Worlds	William's Way
Black Strap Cove	Eastern Beach
Caleta Hotel	
Catalan Bay	
Eastern Beach	
St Theresa's Church	St Theresa's Church
Park & Ride Garage	Faulknor House
Referendum House	Notre Dame School
Constitution House	Glacis Kiosk
Market Place	Market Place
Ocean Village	Waterport Road
Albert Risso House	Sir William Jackson Grove
GASA Swimming Pool	Varyl Begg Estate
St Bernard's Hospital	St Bernard's Hospital
Edinburgh House	
Reclamation Road Terminus	Reclamation Road Terminus

Route 7

↓ Outbound	↑ Inbound
Mount Alvernia Term.	Mount Alvernia Term.
	Old Casino
	Rock Hotel
Trafalgar Cemetery	Eliott's Way
	Referendum Gates
Convent Place	Cathedral Square
NatWest Bank	British War Memorial
Fish Market Steps	Orange Bastion

Route 9

↓ Outbound	↑ Inbound
Rosia Terminus	Rosia Terminus
South Pavilion steps	Rosia Plaza
St Joseph's School	South Gate
New Mole House	New Harbours
Cumberland	Jumper's Building
Jumper's Building	Governor's Meadow House
Victoria House	Alameda House
Trafalgar Cemetery	Referendum Gates
Convent Place	Cathedral Square
King's Bastion	British War Memorial
Fish Market Steps	Orange Bastion
Market Place	Glacis Kiosk
Ocean Village	Market Place
Albert Risso House	
GASA Swimming Pool	Waterport Road
St Bernard's Hospital	Sir William Jackson Grove
Montagu Gardens Terminus	Montagu Gardens Terminus

Route 10

↓ Outbound	↑ Inbound
Frontier/Airport	Frontier/Airport
Referendum House	Referendum House
Constitution House	Constitution House
Ocean Village	Ocean Village
Albert Risso House	Albert Risso House
GASA Swimming Pool	GASA Swimming Pool
St Bernard's Hospital	St Bernard's Hospital
Europort Building	Europort Building
Mid-Harbour	Mid-Harbour
Commonwealth Park	Commonwealth Park
Kings Wharf	Kings Wharf
Queensway Quay	Queensway Quay
Ragged Staff Road	Ragged Staff Road
Boyd Street	Boyd Street

Working as a contractor?

Setting up a limited company in the UK?

Check out this Amazon bestseller from the same author.

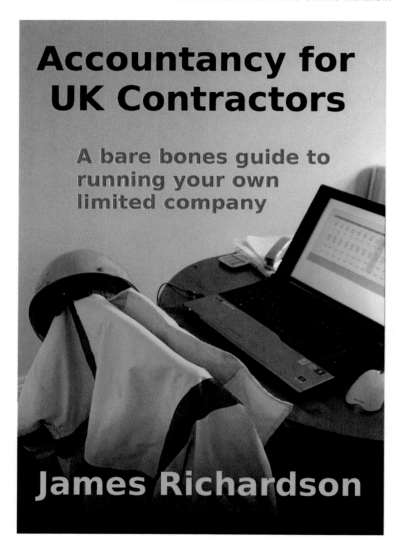

Made in the USA
Las Vegas, NV
27 December 2021

39674837R00036